CHRISTOPHER OKIGBO (1932–1967), who died aged 35 during the Biafran conflict, is regarded by many as the most important African poet of the twentieth century. Stylistically radical, intent on complicating definitions of 'tradition' and 'modernity', and written at a time of epochal socio-political shifts, his work continues to fascinate a wide range of audiences. Born in colonial eastern Nigeria, Okigbo's first poems were written whilst a student at University College, Ibadan, then a hot-bed of intellectual activity. A key figure in the seminal Mbari Club (a collective of writers and artists), Okigbo began to publish widely in 1962, with work appearing in the magazines *Black Orpheus* and *Transition*. In the same year the sequence *Heavensgate* was published by Mbari Publications, who later brought out *Limits* (1964) and *Silences* (1965). In 1968 – towards the end of a decade which saw Nigeria gain its independence – Okigbo published *Paths of Thunder*, again in *Black Orpheus*. United in the posthumously published collection *Labyrinths* (Heinemann, 1971), these various works, composed in less than a decade, comprise a remarkable feat of intellectual and poetic endeavour.

CHIMAMANDA NGOZI ADICHIE is one of the leading voices of a new generation of African writers. Raised in Enugu State, Nigeria, Adichie began her critically acclaimed first work, *Purple Hibiscus*, whilst studying in the United States. Her second novel, *Half of a Yellow Sun*, was published in 2006 and among other awards received the Orange Broadband Prize for Fiction. *The Thing Around Your Neck*, a collection of short stories, was published in 2009. Currently dividing her time between the United States and Nigeria, Adichie is also a noted commentator on the interlinked issues of African identity and migration.

GW00566776

CHRISTOPHER OKIGBO

# LABYRINTHS

INTRODUCTION BY
CHIMAMANDA NGOZI ADICHIE

Heinemann

Pearson Education Limited is a company incorporated in England and Wales, having its registered office at Edinburgh Gate, Harlow, Essex, CM20 2JE.
Registered company number: 872828

*Heavensgate* first published © Mbari, 1962
*Distances* first published in *Transition No. 16*, 1964
*Silences* first published: Part I *Lament of the Silent Sisters* in *Transitions No. 8*, 1963; Part II *Lament of the Drums* © Mbari, 1965
*Path of Thunder* first published in *Black Orpheus,* February, 1968
*Limits* © Christopher Okigbo, 1964

This collection first published in the Heinemann African Writers Series, 1971
Text © Legal Personal representative of Christopher Okigbo, 1971, 2011
This edition published 2011 by Pearson Education Ltd
Introduction © Chimamanda Ngozi Adichie, 2011 All rights reserved

15 14 13 12 11
10 9 8 7 6 5 4 3 2 1

ISBN 978 0 435045 69 2

**British Library Cataloguing in Publication Data**
A catalogue record for this book is available from the British Library.

**Copyright notice**
All rights reserved. No part of this publication may be reproduced
in any form or by any means (including photocopying or storing it in any
medium by electronic means and whether or not transiently or incidentally
to some other use of this publication) without the written permission of the
copyright owner, except in accordance with the provisions of the Copyright,
Designs and Patents Act 1988 or under the terms of a licence issued by the
Copyright Licensing Agency, Saffron House, 6–10 Kirby Street, London
EC1N 8TS (www.cla.co.uk). Applications for the copyright owner's written
permission should be addressed to the publisher.

Typeset by Sara Rafferty
Black and white line illustrations by Demas Nwoko
Cover design by Tony Richardson
Cover photograph © iStockphoto/Srdjan Stefanovic
Author photograph reproduced with the permission of the Christopher
Okigbo Foundation
Printed by Multivista Global Ltd

**Acknowledgements**
Every effort has been made to contact copyright holders of material
reproduced in this book. Any omissions will be rectified in subsequent
printings if notice is given to the publishers.

# CONTENTS

# OKIGBO: AN INTRODUCTION
by Chimamanda Ngozi Adichie

In October 1960, with much fanfare, Nigeria became independent of British rule. Reports in the press emphasised the auspicious signs of what was believed to be the 'Giant of Africa': its educated elite, natural resources, and large population. But the parades masked the dark clouds of a discontent that would manifest itself in political unrest and violence. Barely seven years after independence, following massacres of easteners living in the north, the eastern region seceded from the rest of the country and pronounced itself the independent nation of Biafra. The Nigerian government declared war, and what followed was arguably the darkest chapter of Nigeria's history: a war that left at least a million people dead, towns completely destroyed and a generation stripped of its innocence.

It was, on the Biafran side, a war in which intellectuals, writers and poets actively participated, buoyed by their belief in the secessionist cause. Most of them, like my father, who was a university professor, took on administrative roles in public relations or in organising the war effort. But one young man, by then regarded as one of the best poets of his generation, volunteered for the Biafran Army. He was a Romantic. He wanted to fight for what he believed in. His name was Christopher Okigbo, and he died shortly after the war started, in 1967, in Nsukka. His obituary, written in *Transition*, the most important African literary magazine at the time, and which he co-edited, begins with the words: 'Chris Okigbo is dead, killed by Nigeria.' It was a staggering loss, captured in the words of the literary critic Sunday Anozie, who wrote that 'nothing can be more tragic to the world of African poetry in English than the death of Christopher Okigbo'. Okigbo continues to be mourned by many writers, many of whom have been influenced by his work, such as the critic and academic Ali Mazrui, whose novel *The Trial of Christopher Okigbo* was published in 1971. I was born ten years after the death of Okigbo, the daughter of a man who was Okigbo's contemporary – and forty years after his death, I would write a novel based on the Biafran war in which, haunted by the loss of the poet, I would loosely base a character on him as a tribute to his work and his courage.

Christopher Okigbo was born in 1930 in Ojoto, a village in eastern Nigeria, during a period of great transition in Igboland. After trying for years, the European Christian missionaries had finally set down roots among the Igbo people. The evangelising mission of the churches was aided by the British colonial government, which had, in 1914, created 'Nigeria' from two of its protectorates in West Africa. The missionaries brought schools to which many families sent their children, aware that a western education would be central in the new colonial world. Many struggled to find a balance between the old, familiar, traditional religion of the Igbo and the new Christian religion. Christopher Okigbo's father was of the first generation of Igbo people to convert to Christianity. He became a Roman Catholic and worked as a school teacher, travelling to various towns and villages as an educator in the Catholic schools. Okigbo was born into this world, in which the new co-existed, often uneasily, with the old. He too grew up a Roman Catholic, but was also very much influenced by Igbo religion. Many members of his extended family had not converted to Christianity and it was through them that he learned about the ways of his people, especially about Idoto, an important deity in Ojoto. Reincarnation is a central belief in Igbo cosmology and Okigbo was believed to be the reincarnation of his grandfather, an accomplished and famous man, who came from a line of Idoto priests. Okigbo was, therefore, born into a certain kind of priesthood. This, in addition to other elements of Igbo religion, would greatly influence his work as a poet.

Although quite a few Nigerians had already been western-educated at the turn of the twentieth century, some of them in Europe, Okigbo's was the first generation to benefit from the British colonial government's initial attempt at mass education in Nigeria. In addition to the schools run by the missionaries, the government had also decided to set up a few schools, modelled on English public schools, to train the males to whom the running of the country would be handed over when the British left. Okigbo attended one of those schools, the famous Umuahia Government College, where he was introduced to cricket and to books. He was remembered as charming, sometimes contrarian, and intrepid. He asked questions, and displayed a remarkable confidence. He did not, as yet, show any inclination toward writing. He later attended University College, Ibadan, which, like his secondary school, was at the time a prestigious gathering of men (and a few women) who would play important roles in Nigerian society. Chinua Achebe, who would go on to write the most famous African novel in English, *Things Fall Apart*, was his schoolmate and friend, as was Wole Soyinka, who would go on to win the Nobel Prize in Literature.

Okigbo studied classics. He was a sportsman, played the piano, was sociable and charming. He loved Virgil, and the walls of his university room were covered with hastily scrawled English verses – his attempts at translating the *Aeneid*. After graduating, he worked as a teacher, editor and librarian before he began to write poetry seriously in 1958, at a time when, as he later stated in an interview, 'I found myself wanting to know myself better'. He was very much influenced by Igbo religion, by his childhood experiences, but also by music, and by the French and Spanish poets. When asked in an interview about the influences on his poem 'Heavensgate', he replied, 'I was working under the spell of the Impressionist composers Debussy, César Franck, Ravel.' He was active in the literary life, was one of the founding members of Mbari, a literary club at Ibadan, and served as editor of two important literary journals, while also working on his poetry. By 1962, he had completed 'Limits' and 'Heavensgate', the two sequences collected here as *Labyrinths*.

My first introduction to Christopher Okigbo's work was in the mid-1990s, in my secondary school literature class in Nsukka, the same town where he was killed in battle. We had studied poems by Senghor and Wordsworth, but the only poem my teacher wanted us to memorise was Christopher Okigbo's 'Heavensgate'. It was clear that he thought Okigbo's work was not only worth memorising, but somehow different from the other poems we had studied.

> Before you, mother Idoto,
> naked I stand,
> before your watery presence,
> a prodigal.

I can still recite it by heart. I did not understand it, did not find the academic 'meaning' I had been taught to look for in poems, but it was also the only poem that left me with a strange feeling, a shiver of recognition. Some of Okigbo's poems were cryptic, but also mysterious in a way that promised to reward re-reading, with layered allusions, and with a kind of feeling and emotion and truth.

In a 1962 interview, Okigbo said, 'I don't need applause.' He had no ambition, he claimed, to be a great writer or even a popular writer. But he has become THE most talked about poet of his generation, a cult hero whose life, death and work remain passionate subjects for many African intellectuals. Not only are young students all over the African continent memorising Okigbo, but young poets are heavily influenced by him. The applause continues.

Although these poems were written and published separately, they are, in fact, organically related.

*Heavensgate* was originally conceived as an Easter sequence. It later grew into a ceremony of innocence, something like a mass, an offering to Idoto, the village stream of which I drank, in which I washed, as a child; the celebrant, a personage like Orpheus, is about to begin a journey. Cleansing involves total nakedness, a complete self-surrender to the water spirit that nurtures all creation. The various sections of the poem, therefore, present this celebrant at various stations of his cross.

*Limits* and *Distances* are man's outer and inner worlds projected – the phenomenal and the imaginative, not in terms of their separateness but of their relationship – an attempt to reconcile the universal opposites of life and death in a live-die proposition: one is the other and either is both.

'Siren Limits' presents a protagonist in pursuit of the white elephant. In his progression to a sacred waterfront he falls victim to his own demonic obsession, becomes disembodied or loses his second self. 'Fragments out of the deluge' renders in retrospect certain details of the protagonist and of his milieu – the collective rape of innocence and profanation of the mysteries, in atonement for which he has had to suffer immolation. (*Limits* was written at the end of a journey of several centuries from Nsukka to Yola in pursuit of what turned out to be an illusion.)

*Distances* is, on the other hand, a poem of homecoming, but of homecoming in its spiritual and psychic aspect. The quest broken off after 'Siren Limits' is resumed, this time in the unconscious. The self that suffers, that experiences, ultimately finds fulfilment in a form of psychic union with the supreme spirit that is both destructive and creative. The process is one of sensual anaesthesia, of total liberation from all physical and emotional tension; the end result, a state of aesthetic grace. (*Distances* was written after my first experience of surgery under general anaesthesia.)

Between *Limits* and *Distances* an interval, *Silences*, is provided, in which two groups of mourners explore the possibilities of poetic metaphor in an attempt to elicit the music to which all imperishable cries must aspire. Both parts of *Silences* were inspired by the events of the day: *Lament of the Silent Sisters*, by the Western Nigeria Crisis of 1962, and the death of Patrice Lumumba; *Lament of the Drums*, by the imprisonment of Obafemi Awolowo, and the tragic death of his eldest son.

The 'Silent Sisters' are, however, sometimes like the drowning Franciscan nuns of Hopkins' *The Wreck of the Deutschland*, sometimes like the 'Sirenes' of Debussy's *Nocturne* – two dissonant dreams associated in the dominant motif 'NO in thunder' (from one of Melville's letters to Hawthorne). This motif is developed by a series of related airs from sources as diverse as Malcolm Cowley, Raja Ratnam, Stephane Mallarmé, Rabindranath Tagore, Garçia Lorca and the yet unpublished Peter Thomas – airs which enable the 'Silent Sisters' to evoke, quite often by calling wolf, consonant tunes in life and letters. Section I, for instance, erects an illusion, a storm-tossed ship at mid-sea. The image of drowning virgins, and the dream of ultimate martyrdom are, however, also present. The illusion is enlarged by the motif of carrion-comfort (from one of Hopkins' poems). Section II develops this latter motif in the image of flies and splintered flames gloating over carrion. The chorus breaks into a 'swan song' in Section III; and in the alternation (Section IV) between the Crier and the Chorus the sea herself, hidden face of the dream, is celebrated in her many colours. In Section V the main actors in the events of the day become almost recognizable in the opening couplets. The problem 'How does one say NO in thunder' is then finally resolved in silence. For the ultimate answer is to be sought only in terms of each poet's response to his medium.

The long-drums are, on the other hand, the spirits of the ancestors, the dead. They begin their lament by invoking the elements which make them up, and imploring evil forces to stay away from the rostrum. In Section II, the drums enter their theme song. They are coming out of their place of confinement, 'soot chamber', 'cinerary tower' (1st strophe), not to rejoice but to lament (2nd strophe). They are like urgent telegrams which are dispatched only when tragic events happen (3rd strophe). 'Babylonian capture', 'martyrdom' and 'chaliced vintage' suggest that someone might have been betrayed by his disciples (5th strophe). The alternation (in Section III) between the horns of elephant tusks (the italicised passages) and the drums establishes an identity between the personage of Section II, and Palinurus, the helmsman of Aeneas' ship during his legendary voyage to Italy. In Section IV, the drums return to their theme song, weary and exhausted from the long excursion of Section III. After a few limbering-up passages (1st, 2nd and 3rd strophes) a treble drum takes a six-phrase solo (4th strophe). A six-phrase response by the mother-of-drums (5th strophe) leads on to the re-entry of the horns in a variation on Ishthar's lament for Tammuz (Section V). Here the theme of the poem is no longer suggested but stated; the personages of the earlier sections together become fused with that of Tammuz, and consequently with the movement of the seasons.

*Labyrinths* is thus a fable of man's perennial quest for fulfilment. (The title may suggest Minos' legendary palace at Cnossus, but the double headed axe is as much a symbol of sovereignty in traditional Ibo society as in Crete. Besides, the long and tortuous passage to the shrine of the 'long-juju' of the Aro Ibos may, perhaps, best be described as a labyrinth.) Inevitably, several presences haunt the complex of rooms and ante-rooms, of halls and corridors that lead to the palace of the White Goddess, and in which a country visitor might easily lose his way. Nevertheless, a poet-protagonist is assumed throughout; a personage, however, much larger than Orpheus; one with a load of destiny on his head, rather like Gilgamesh, like Aeneas, like the hero of Melville's *Moby Dick*, like the Fisher King of Eliot's *Waste Land*; a personage for whom the progression through 'Heavensgate' through 'Limits' through 'Distances' is like telling the beads of a rosary; except that the beads are neither stone nor agate but globules of anguish strung together on memory.

Every work of this kind is necessarily a cry of anguish – of the root extending its branches of coral, of corals extending their roots into each living hour; the swell of the silent sea the great heaving dream at its highest, the thunder of splitting pods – the tears scatter, take root, the cotyledons broken, burgeon into laughter of leaf; or else rot into vital hidden roles in the nitrogen cycle. The present dream clamoured to be born a cadenced cry: silence to appease the fever of flight beyond the iron gate.

*Christopher Okigbo*
Ibadan
October 1965

*For*
*Safinat and Ibrahimat*
*mother and child*

# ACKNOWLEDGEMENTS

For permission to reprint I am grateful to the editor of *Transition* in which the earliest versions of 'Limits', 'Silences' and 'Distances' made their first public appearance; and to Mbari Publications under whose imprint *Heavensgate* (1962), *Limits* (1964) and *Silences* (1965) have previously been published. The versions here preserved are, however, somewhat different and are final.

I am also grateful to novelists Chinua Achebe and Dennis Williams, critics Ulli Beier and Gerald Moore, for constant interest and encouragement; to critic Sunday Anozie, and poet Paul Theroux, who share with me the experience of *Labyrinths*; and to Benedict Obumselu for criticisms that continue to guide me along the paths of greater clarity.

*Christopher Okigbo*

*Heavensgate*

*Initiations*

*Watermaid*

*Newcomer*

# Heavensgate

# I *The Passage*

BEFORE YOU, mother Idoto,[*]
  naked I stand;
before your watery presence,
  a prodigal

leaning on an oilbean,
lost in your legend.

Under your power wait I
  on barefoot,
watchman for the watchword
  at *Heavensgate*;

out of the depths my cry:
give ear and hearken . . .

[*]A village stream. The oilbean, the tortoise and the python are totems for her worship.

DARK WATERS of the beginning.

Rays, violet and short, piercing the gloom,
foreshadow the fire that is dreamed of.

Rainbow on far side, arched like boa bent to kill,
foreshadows the rain that is dreamed of.

Me to the orangery
solitude invites,
a wagtail, to tell
the tangled-wood-tale;
a sunbird, to mourn
a mother on a spray.

Rain and sun in single combat;
on one leg standing,
in silence at the passage,
the young bird at the passage.

SILENT FACES at crossroads:
   festivity in black . . .

Faces of black like long black
   column of ants,

behind the bell tower,
into the hot garden
where all roads meet:
festivity in black . . .

O Anna at the knobs of the panel oblong,
hear us at crossroads at the great hinges

where the players of loft pipe organs
rehearse old lovely fragments, alone –

strains of pressed orange leaves on pages,
bleach of the light of years held in leather:

For we are listening in cornfields
   among the windplayers,
listening to the wind leaning over
   its loveliest fragment . . .

## II *Initiations*

SCAR OF the crucifix
over the breast,
by red blade inflicted
by red-hot blade,
on right breast witnesseth

mystery which I, initiate,
received newly naked
upon waters of the genesis
from Kepkanly.*

Elemental, united in vision
of present and future,
the pure line, whose innocence
denies inhibitions.

At confluence of planes, the angle:
man loses man, loses vision;

so comes John the Baptist
with bowl of salt water
preaching the gambit:
life without sin, without

life; which accepted,
way leads downward
down orthocenter
avoiding decisions.

* A half-serious half-comical primary school teacher of the late
  thirties.

6

Or forms fourth angle –
duty, obligation:

square yields the moron,
fanatics and priests and popes,
organizing secretaries and
party managers; better still,

the rhombus – brothers and deacons,
liberal politicians,
selfish selfseekers – all who are good
doing nothing at all;

the quadrangle, the rest, me and you . . .

Mystery, which barring
the errors of the rendering
witnesseth
red-hot blade on right breast
the scar of the crucifix.

and the hand fell with Haragin,[*]
Kepkanly that wielded the blade;

with Haragin with God's light between them:

but the solitude within me remembers Kepkanly . . .

[*] Kepkanly was reported to have died from excess of joy when he
received arrears of salary awarded by the Haragin Commission
of 1945.

AND THIS from Jadum,*

(Say if thou knowest
from smell of the incense
a village where liveth
in the heart of the grassland
a minstrel who singeth)

to shepherds, with a lute on his lip:

Do not wander in speargrass,
After the lights,
Probing lairs in stockings,
To roast
The viper alive, with dog lying
Upsidedown in the crooked passage . . .

Do not listen at keyholes,
After the lights,
To smell from other rooms,
After the lights –

Singeth Jadum from Rockland,
after the lights.

And there are here
the errors of the rendering . . .

* A half-demented village minstrel

AND THIS from Upandru:*

Screen your bedchamber thoughts
with sun-glasses,
who could jump your eye,
your mind-window,

And I said:
The prophet only the poet.
And he said: Logistics.
(Which is what poetry is) . . .

And he said to the ram: Disarm.
And I said:
Except by rooting,
who could pluck yam tubers from their base?

And there are here
the errors of the rendering . . .

* A village explainer

9

### III *Watermaid*

EYE OPEN on the sea,
eyes open, of the prodigal;
upward to heaven shoot
where stars will fall from.

Secret I have told into no ear,
save into a dughole, to hold, not to drown with –
Secret I have planned into beachsand

now breaks
salt-white surf on the stones and me,
and lobsters and shells
in iodine smell –
maid of the salt-emptiness,
sophisticreamy,

whose secret I have covered up with beachsand . . .

Shadow of rain over sunbeaten beach,
shadow of rain over man with woman.

BRIGHT
with the armpit-dazzle of a lioness,
she answers,

wearing white light about her;

and the waves escort her,
my lioness,
crowned with moonlight.

So brief her presence –
match-flare in wind's breath –
so brief with mirrors around me.

Downward . . .
the waves distil her;
gold crop
sinking ungathered.

Watermaid of the salt-emptiness,
grown are the ears of the secret.

AND I WHO am here abandoned,

count the sand by wavelash abandoned,
count her blessing, my white queen.

But the spent sea reflects
from his mirrored visage
not my queen, a broken shadow.

So I who count in my island the moments,
count the hour which will bring

my lost queen with angels' ash in the wind.

THE STARS have departed,
the sky in monocle
surveys the worldunder.

The stars have departed,
and I – where am I?

Stretch, stretch, O antennae,
to clutch at this hour,

fulfilling each moment in a
broken monody.

# **IV** *Lustra*

so WOULD I to the hills again
so would I
to where springs the fountain
there to draw from

And to hill top clamber
body and soul
whitewashed in the moondew
there to see from

So would I from my eye the mist
so would I
thro' moonmist to hilltop
there for the cleansing

Here is a new laid egg
here a white hen at midterm.

THE FLOWER weeps, unbruised,
for him who was silenced
whose advent dumb-bells celebrate
in dim light with wine song:

*Messiah will come again*
*After the argument in heaven*
*Messiah will come again …*

Fingers of penitence bring
to a palm grove
vegetable offering with five
fingers of chalk …

THUNDERING drums and cannons
in palm grove:
the spirit is in ascent.

I have visited;
on palm beam imprinted
my pentagon –

I have visited, the prodigal ...

In palm grove,
long-drums and cannons:
the spirit in the ascent.

**V** *Newcomer*

TIME for worship –

softly sing the bells of exile,
the angelus,
softly sings my guardian angel.

Mask over my face –

my own mask, not ancestral – I sign:
remembrance of calvary,
and of age of innocence, which is of . . .

Time for worship:

*Anna of the panel oblongs,*
    *protect me*
*from them fucking angels;*
    *protect me*
*my sandhouse and bones.*

*For Georgette*

IN THE CHILL breath of the day's waking,
comes the newcomer,

when the draper of May
has sold out fine green garments,

and the hillsides have made up their faces,
and the gardens, on their faces a painted smile:

such synthetic welcome at the cock's third siren;
when from behind the bulrushes

waking, in the teeth of the chill May morn,
comes the newcomer.

I AM standing above the noontide,
Above the bridgehead;

Listening to the laughter of waters
   that do not know why:

Listening to incense –

I am standing above the noontide
   with my head above it;

Under my feet float the waters
Tide blows them under . . .

# *Limits*

## *Limits* **I–IV:**
**Siren Limits**


SUDDENLY becoming talkative
   like weaverbird
Summoned at offside of
   dream remembered

Between sleep and walking,
I hang up my egg-shells
To you of palm grove,
Upon whose bamboo towers

Hang, dripping with yesterupwine,
A tiger mask and nude spear . . .

Queen of the damp half light,
I have had my cleansing,
Emigrant with air-borne nose,
The he-goat-on-heat.

## II

FOR HE WAS a shrub among the poplars,
Needing more roots
More sap to grow to sunlight,
Thirsting for sunlight,

A low growth among the forest.

Into the soul
The selves extended their branches,
Into the moments of each living hour,
Feeling for audience

Straining thin among the echoes;

And out of the solitude
Voice and soul with selves unite,
Riding the echoes,

Horsemen of the apocalypse;

And crowned with one self
The name displays its foliage,
Hanging low

A green cloud above the forest.

# III

BANKS OF reed.
Mountains of broken bottles.

*& the mortar is not yet dry …*

Silent the footfall,
Soft as cat's paw,
Sandalled in velvet fur,

So we must go, eve-mist on shoulders,
Sun's dust of combat,
With brand burning out at hand-end.

*& the mortar is not yet dry …*

Then we must sing, tongue-tied,
Without name or audience,
Making harmony among the branches.

And this is the crisis point,
The twilight moment between
   sleep and waking;
And voice that is reborn transpires,
Not thro' pores in the flesh,
   but the soul's back-bone.

Hurry on down –
  Thro' the high-arched gate –
Hurry on down
  little stream to the lake;

Hurry on down –
  Thro' the cinder market –
Hurry on down
  in the wake of the dream;

Hurry on down –
  To rockpoint of Cable,*

To pull by the rope
  the big white elephant . . .

*& the mortar is not yet dry*
*& the mortar is not yet dry;*

And the dream wakes
  the voice fades
In the damp half light
  like a shadow,

Not leaving a mark.

---

* Cable Point at Asaba, a sacred waterfront with rocky promontory,
  and terminal point of a traditional quinquennial pilgrimage.

# IV

AN IMAGE insists
From flag pole of the heart;
Her image distracts
With the cruelty of the rose . . .

Oblong-headed lioness –
No shield is proof against her –
Wound me, O sea-weed
Face, blinded like strong-room –

Distances of her armpit-fragrance
Turn chloroform enough for my patience –

When you have finished
& done up my stitches,
Wake me near the altar,
& this poem will be finished . . .

## *Limits* **V–XII:**
## **Fragments out of the Deluge**

ON AN empty sarcophagus
   hewn out of alabaster,
A branch of fennel on an
   empty sarcophagus* ...

Nothing suggests accident
   where the beast†
Is finishing her rest ...

Smoke of ultramarine and amber
Floats above the fields after
Moonlit rains, from tree unto tree
Distils the radiance of a king‡ ...

You might as well see the new branch of Enkidu;§
And that is no new thing either ...

---

* The body of one of the Egyptian Pharaohs is said to have
   metamorphosed into a fennel branch.
† The lioness of LIMITS IV who destroyed the hero's second self.
‡ The hero is like Gilgamesh, legendary king of Uruk in
   Mesopotamia, and first human hero in literature.
§ Companion and second self of Gilgamesh.

28

# VI

HE STOOD in the midst of them all
  and appeared in true form,
He found them drunken, he found none
  thirsty among them.

*Who would add to your statue,*
*Or in your village accept you?*

He fed them on seed wrapped in wonders;
They deemed it a truth-value system,
  Man out of innocence,
And there was none thirsty among them.

They cast him in mould of iron,
And asked him to do a rock-drill –
  Man out of innocence –
He drilled with dumb-bells about him.

And they took the key off
And they hid the key of . . .
That none may enter.

And they took the hot spoils off the battle,
And they shared the hot spoils among them:

Estates, among them;
And they were the chosen,
  mongrel breeds,
With slogan in hand, of
  won divination . . .

And you talk of the people:
There is none thirsty among them.

29

## VII

And from frame of iron,
And in mould of iron . . .

*For he ate the dead lion,*
*& was within the corpse –*

Which is not the point;
And who says it matters
Which way the kite flows,
Provided the movement is
Around the burning market –

  And lilies
Sprouted from rosebeds,
  Canalilies,
Like tombstones from pavements;

And to the cross in the void came pilgrims;
Came, floating with burnt-out tapers;

Past the village orchard where
Flannagan*
Preached the Pope's message,
To where drowning nuns suspired,
Asking the key-word from stone;
& he said:

*To sow the fireseed among grasses,*
*& lo, to keep it till it burns out ...*

* A well-known Irish priest of the 1940s.

# VIII

BUT THE sunbird repeats
Over the oilbean shadows:

'A fleet of eagles,
  over the oilbean shadows,
Holds the square
  under curse of their breath.

Beaks of bronze, wings
  of hard-tanned felt,
The eagles flow
  over man-mountains,
Steep walls of voices,
  horizons;
The eagles furrow
  dazzling over the voices
With wings like
  combs in the wind's hair

Out of the solitude, the fleet,
Out of the solitude,
Intangible like silk thread of sunlight,
The eagles ride low,
Resplendent ... resplendent;
And small birds sing in shadows,
Wobbling under their bones ...'

## IX

AND, squatting,
A blind dog* howls at his godmother:

Eunice† at the passageway,
Singing the moon to sleep over the hills,
Eunice at the passageway …

Give him no chair, they say,
The dawn's charioteer,
Riding with the angry stars
Toward the great sunshine.

---

* Known for his power of prophecy.
† My childhood nurse known for her lyricism.

‡ The tortoise and the python.
§ In Sumerian myth, queen of the underworld.

# X

AND TO US they came –
*Malisons, malisons, mair than ten –*
And climbed the bombax
And killed the Sunbird.

And they scanned the forest of oilbean,
Its approach; surveyed its high branches ...

And they entered into the forest,
And they passed through the forest of oilbean
And found them, the twin-gods[‡] of the forest ...

And the beasts broke –
*Mailsons, malisons, mair than ten –*
And dawn-gust grumbled,
Fanning the grove
Like a horse-tail-man,
Like handmaid of dancers,
Fanning their branches.

Their talons they drew out of their scabbard,
Upon the tree trunks, as if on fire-clay,
Their beaks they sharpened;
And spread like eagles their felt-wings,
And descended upon the twin gods of Irkalla[§]

And the ornaments of him,
And the beads about his tail;
And the carapace of her,
And her shell, they divided.

# XI

AND THE gods lie in state
And the gods lie in state
Without the long-drum.

And the gods lie unsung,
Veiled only with mould,
Behind the shrinehouse.

Gods grow out,
Abandoned;
And so do they . . .

# XII

BUT AT THE window, outside, a shadow:

The sunbird sings again
From the LIMITS of the dream;
The Sunbird sings again
Where the caress does not reach,

   *of Guernica,*\*
On whose canvas of blood,
The slits of his tongue
   cling to glue . . .

*& the cancelling out is complete.*

\* A work by Picasso.

*Silences*

**Lament of the Silent Sisters**
**Lament of the Drums**

## Lament of the Silent Sisters
## I

Crier:     IS THERE ... Is certainly there ...
             For as in sea-fever globules of fresh anguish
                immense golden eggs empty of albumen
                sink into our balcony ...

             How does one say NO in thunder . . .

             For in breakers in sea-fever compass or cross
                makes a difference: certainly makes
                not an escape ladder . . .

             Where is there for us an anchorage;
             A shank for a sheet, a double arch –

Chorus:  They comb the afternoon the scavengers
             For scented shadows above the underrush –

Crier:     The cross to us we still call to us,
             In this jubilee-dance above the carrion ...

## II

Chorus:  THIS SHADOW of carrion incites
    and in rhythms of silence
Urges us; gathers up our broken
    hidden feather-of-flight,
To this anguished cry of Moloch:

What cast-iron steps cascading down the valley
    all forged into thunder of tanks;
And detonators cannoned into splintered flames,
    in this jubilee-dance of fireflies!

Crier:  They struck him in the ear they struck him in the
eye;
They picked his bones for scavenging:

Chorus:  And there will be continual going to the well,
Until they smash their calabashes.

Crier:  So, one dips one's tongue in ocean, and begins
To cry to the mushroom of the sky:

# III

*Chorus:*   DUMB-BELLS outside the gates
             In hollow seascapes without memory, we carry
             Each of us an urn of native
             Earth, a double handful anciently gathered.

             And by salt mouths by yellow
             Sand banks sprinkled with memories, we spread
             To the nightairs our silences,
             Suffused in this fragrance of divers melodies:

*Crier:*    This is our swan song
             This is our senses' stillness:

*Chorus:*   We carry in our worlds that flourish
             Our worlds that have failed . . .

*Crier:*    This is our swan song
             This is the sigh of our spirits:

*Chorus:*   Unseen shadows like long-fingered winds
             Pluck from our strings
             This shriek, the music of the firmament . . .

## IV

*Alternatively*
*Crier/Chorus:*

I SEE many colours in the salt teeth of foam

Which is no where to face under the half-light

The rainbow they say is full of harmonies

We shall make a grey turn to face it.

Wild winds cry out against us

We shall swallow our heart in our stomach

More wrinkles on the salt face of glass

The winds' broom sweeps only the surface.

I hear many voices about us

We shall wear the green habit of kolanuts

The kingfisher gathers his ropes in the distance

The salt water gathers them inward

The dipping paddle blades, the inconstant
dolphins

The salt water gathers them inward.

Will the water gather us in her sibylline chamber?

And our silences fade into galloping antelopes?

# V

*Alternatively*
*Crier/Chorus:*

YELLOW images:
Voices in the senses' stillness ...

Pointed arches:
Pieces in the form of a pear ...

Angles, filaments:
Hosts of harlequins in the shadows:

And bearded Judas,
Resplendent among the dancers ...

I hear sounds as, they say,
A worshipper hears the flutes –

The music sounds so in the soul
It can hear nothing else –

I hear painted harmonies
From the mushroom of the sky –

Silences are melodies
Heard in retrospect:

And how does one say NO in thunder?

One dips one's tongue in the ocean;
Camps with the choir of inconstant
Dolphins, by shallow sand banks
Sprinkled with memories;
Extends one's branches of coral,
The branches extends in the senses'
Silence; this silence distills
in yellow melodies.

## Lament of the Drums
## I

LION-HEARTED cedar forest, gonads for our thunder,
Even if you are very far away, we invoke you:

Give us our hollow heads of long-drums ...

Antelopes for the cedar forest, swifter messengers
Than flash-of-beacon-flame, we invoke you:

Hide us; deliver us from our nakedness ...

Many-fingered canebrake, exile for our laughter,
Even if you are very far away, we invoke you:

Come; limber our raw hides of antelopes ...

Thunder of tanks of giant iron steps of detonators,
Fail safe from the clearing, we implore you:

We are tuned for a feast-of-seven-souls ...

## II

AND THE DRUMS once more
From our soot chamber,
From the cinerary tower
To the crowded clearing;

Long-drums, we awake
Like a shriek of incense,
The unheard sullen shriek
Of the funerary ram:

Liquid messengers of blood,
Like urgent telegrams,
We have never been deployed
For feast of antelopes ...

And to the Distant – but how shall we go?
The robbers will strip us of our tendons!

For we sense
With dog-nose a Babylonian capture,
The martyrdom
Blended into that chaliced vintage;

And savour
The incense and in high buskin,
Like a web
Of voices all rent by javelins.

But distant seven winds invite us and our cannons
To limber our membranes for a dance of elephants ...

# III

THEY ARE FISHING *today in the dark waters*
*Where the mariner is finishing his rest ...*

Palinurus, alone in a hot prison, you will keep
The dead sea awake with nightsong ...

*Silver of rivulets this side of the bridge,*
*Cascades of lily-livered laughter,*
*Fold-on-fold of raped, naked blue –*
*What memory has the sea of her lover?*

Palinurus, unloved in your empty catacomb,
You will wear away through age alone ...

*Nothing remains, only smoke after storm –*
*Some strange Celaeno and her harpy crew,*
*Laden with night and their belly's excrement,*
*Profane all things with hooked feet and foul teeth –*

Masks and beggar-masks without age or shadow:
Broken tin-gods whose vision is dissolved ...

*It is over, Palinurus, at least for you,*
*In your tarmac of night and fever-dew;*

*Tears of grace, not of sorrow, broken*
*In two, protest your inviolable image;*

*And the sultry waters, touched by the sun,*
*Inherit your paleness who reign, resigned*

Like palm oil fostered in an ancient clay bowl;
A half-forgotten name; like a stifled sneeze ...

*Fishermen out there in the dark – O you*
*Who rake the waves or chase their wake –*
*Weave for him a shadow out of your laughter*
*For a dumb child to hide his nakedness ...*

# IV

AND THE DRUMS
Once more and like masked dancers,
On the orange –
Yellow myth of the sands of exile –

Long-drums dis-
Jointed, and with bleeding tendons,
Like tarantulas
Emptied of their bitterest poisons,

And to the Distant – but how shall we go?
The robbers will strip us of our thunder ...

– So, like a dead letter unanswered,
  Our rococo
  Choir of insects is null
  Cacophony
  And void as a debt summons served
  On a bankrupt;

– But the antiphony, still clamorous,
  In tremolo,
  Like an afternoon, for shadows;
  And the winds
  The distant seven cannons invite us
  To a sonorous

Ishthar's lament for Tammuz:

## V

FOR THE FAR *removed there is wailing:*

For the far removed;
For the Distant ...

*The wailing is for the fields of crop:*

The drums' lament is:
They grow not ...

*The wailing is for the fields of men:*

For the barren wedded ones;
For perishing children ...

*The wailing is for the Great River:*

Her pot-bellied watchers
Despoil her ...

*Distances*

# I

FROM FLESH into phantom on the horizontal stone
I was the sole witness to my homecoming ...

Serene lights on the other balcony:
redolent fountains bristling with signs –

But what does my divine rejoicing hold?
A bowl of incense, a nest of fireflies?

I was the sole witness to my homecoming ...

For in the inflorescence of the white
chamber, a voice, from very far away,
chanted, and the chamber descanted, the birthday of earth,
paddled me home through some dark
labyrinth, from laughter to the dream.

Miner into my solitude,
incarnate voice of the dream,
you will go,
with me as your chief acolyte,
again into the anti-hill ...

I was the sole witness to my homecoming ...

## II

DEATH LAY in ambush that evening in that island;
voice sought its echo that evening in that island.

And the eye lost its light,
the light lost its shadow.

For the wind, eternal suitor of dead leaves,
unrolled his bandages to the finest swimmer ...

It was an evening without flesh or skeleton;
an evening with no silver bells to its tale;
without lanterns, an evening without buntings;
and it was an evening without age or memory –

for we are talking of such commonplaces,
and on the brink of such great events ...

And in the freezing tuberoses of the white
chamber, eyes that had lost their animal
colour, havoc of eyes of incandescent rays,
pinned me, cold, to the marble stretcher,

until my eyes lost their blood
and the blood lost its odour,

and the everlasting fire from the oblong window
forgot the taste of ash in the air's marrow:

anguish and solitude …
Smothered, my scattered
cry, the dancers,
lost among their own
snares; the faces,
the hands held captive;
the interspaces
reddening with blood;

and behind them all,
in smock of white cotton,
Death herself,
the chief celebrant,
in a cloud of incense,
paring her fingernails …

At her feet rolled their heads like cut fruits;
about her fell
their severed members, numerous as locusts.

Like split wood left to dry, the dismembered
joints of the ministrants piled high.

She bathed her knees in the blood of attendants;
her smock in entrails of ministrants …

## III

IN THE scattered line of pilgrims
bound for Shibboleth
in my hand the crucifix
the torn branch the censer

In the scattered line of pilgrims
from Dan to Beersheeba
camphor iodine chloroform
either sting me in the bum

On the stone steps on the marble
beyond the balcony
prophets martyrs lunatics
like the long stride of the evening

At the clearing dantini
in the garden dillettanti;
vendors princes negritude
politicians in the tall wood …

## IV

AND AT THE archway
a triangular lintel
of solid alabaster
enclosed in a square
inscribed in a circle
with a hollow centre,
above the archway
yawning shutterless
like celestial pincers
like a vast countenance:

    *the only way to go*
    *through the marble archway*
    *to the catatonic pingpong*
    *of the evanescent halo ...*

And beyond the archway
like pentecostal orbs
resplendent far distant
in the intangible void
an immense crucifix
of phosphorescent mantles:

    *after we had formed*
    *then only the forms were formed*
    *and all the forms*
    *were formed after our forming ...*

## V

SWEAT OVER hoof in ascending gestures –
each step is the step of the mule in the abyss –
the archway the oval the panel oblong
to that sanctuary at the earth's molten bowel
for the music woven into the funerary rose
the water in the tunnel its effervescent laughter
the open laughter of the grape or vine
the question in the inkwell the answer on the monocle
the unanswerable question in the tabernacle's silence –

Censers, from the cradle,
of a nameless religion:

each sigh is time's stillness, in the abyss …

Mated and sealed
in a proud oblation,

brothers to silence and the wandering rocks;

with the burden of the pawn,
on the molten stone,

and the scar of the kiss and of the two swords.

Sweat over hoof
in the settled abyss:

each sigh is the stillness of the kiss …

# VI

THE SEASON the season
the tall wood the clearing
the season the season
the stone steps the dream ...

*Come into my cavern,*
*Shake the mildew from your hair;*
*Let your ear listen:*
*My mouth calls from a cavern ...*

Lo, it is the same blood that flows ...

Shadows distances labyrinths violences,
Skeletal oblong
of my sentient being, I receive you
in my perforated
mouth of a stranger empty of meaning,
stones without juice –

the goat still knows its fodder,
the leopards on its trail –

For it is the same blood,
through the same orifices,
the same branches
trembling intertwined,
and the same faces
in the interspaces.

And it is the same breath, liquid, without acolyte,
like invisible mushrooms on stone surfaces.

And at this chaste instant of delineated anguish,
the same voice, importunate, aglow with the goddess –

unquenchable, yellow, darkening homeward
like a cry of wolf above crumbling houses –

strips the dream naked,
bares the entrails;

and in the orangery of immense corridors,
I wash my feet in your pure head, O maid,

and walk along your feverish, solitary shores,

seeking, among your variegated teeth,
the tuberose of my putrescent laughter:

I have fed out of the drum
I have drunk out of the cymbal

I have entered your bridal
chamber; and lo,

I am the sole witness to my homecoming.

*Path of Thunder*

## Thunder can break

FANFARE of drums, wooden bells: iron chapter;
And our dividing airs are gathered home.

This day belongs to a miracle of thunder;
Iron has carried the forum
With token gestures. Thunder has spoken,
Left no signatures: broken

Barbicans alone tell one tale the winds scatter.

Mountain or tower in sight, lo, your hostages –
Iron has made, alas, masterpieces –
Statuettes of legendary heroes – iron birds
Held – fruit of flight – tight;

For barricaded in iron handiwork a miracle caged.

Bring them out we say, bring them out
Faces and hands and feet,
The stories behind the myth, the plot
Which the ritual enacts.

Thunder can break – Earth, bind me fast –
Obduracy, the disease of elephants.

## Elegy of the Wind

WHITE LIGHT, receive me your sojourner; O milky way,
   let me clasp you to my waist;
And may my muted tones of twilight
Break your iron gate, the burden of several centuries,
   into twin tremulous cotyledons ...

Man of iron throat – for I will make broadcast with
   eunuch-horn of seven valves –
I will follow the wind to the clearing,
And with muffled steps seemingly out of breath break
   the silence the myth of her gate.

For I have lived the sapling sprung from the bed
   of the old vegetation;
Have shouldered my way through a mass of ancient
   nights to chlorophyll;

Or leaned upon a withered branch,
A blind beggar leaning on a porch.

I have lived the oracle dry on the cradle of a new generation ...
The autocycle leans on a porch, the branch dissolves into
                              embers,

The ashes resolve their moments
Of twin-drops of dew on a leaf:
And like motion into stillness is my divine rejoicing –
The man embodies the child
The child embodies the man; the man remembers
The song of the innocent,
Of the uncircumcised at the sight of the flaming razor –

The chief priest of the sanctuary has uttered
   the enchanted words;
The bleeding phallus,
Dripping fresh from the carnage cries out for
   the medicinal leaf ...

O wind, swell my sails; and may my banner run
   the course of wider waters:

The child in me trembles before the high shelf
   on the wall,
The man in me shrinks before the narrow neck of
   a calabash;

And the chant, already all wings, follows
In its ivory circuit behind the thunder clouds,
The slick route of the feathered serpent ...

## Come Thunder

NOW THAT the triumphant march has entered the last street
corners,
Remember, O dancers, the thunder among the clouds ...

Now that laughter, broken in two, hangs tremulous between
the teeth,
Remember, O dancers, the lightning beyond the earth ...

The smell of blood already floats in the lavender-mist of the
afternoon.
The death sentence lies in ambush along the corridors of
power;
And a great fearful thing already tugs at the cables of the open
air,
A nebula immense and immeasurable, a night of deep waters –
An iron dream unnamed and unprintable, a path of stone.

The drowsy heads of the pods in barren farmlands witness it,
The homesteads abandoned in this century's brush fire witness
it:
The myriad eyes of deserted corn cobs in burning barns witness
it:
Magic birds with the miracle of lightning flash on their
feathers ...

The arrows of God tremble at the gates of light,
The drums of curfew pander to a dance of death;

And the secret thing in its heaving
Threatens with iron mask
The last lighted torch of the century ...

## Hurrah for Thunder

WHATEVER happened to the elephant –
Hurrah for thunder –

The elephant, tetrarch of the jungle:
With a wave of the hand
He could pull four trees to the ground;
His four mortar legs pounded the earth:
Wherever they treaded,
The grass was forbidden to be there.

Alas! the elephant has fallen –
Hurrah for thunder –

But already the hunters are talking about pumpkins:
If they share the meat let them remember thunder.

The eye that looks down will surely see the nose;
The finger that fits should be used to pick the nose.

Today – for tomorrow, today becomes yesterday:
How many million promises can ever fill a basket ...

If I don't learn to shut my mouth I'll soon go to hell,
I, Okigbo, town-crier, together with my iron bell.

## Elegy for Slit-drum
### With rattles accompaniment

CONDOLENCES ... from our swollen lips laden with
                                        condolences:
The mythmaker accompanies us
The rattles are here with us

condolences from our split-tongue of the slit drum
                                        condolences

one tongue full of fire
one tongue full of stone –

condolences from the twin-lips of our drum parted in
                                        condolences:
the panther has delivered a hare
the hare is beginning to leap
the panther has delivered a hare
the panther is about to pounce –

condolences already in flight under the burden of this
                                        century:

parliament has gone on leave
the members are now on bail
parliament is now on sale
the voters are lying in wait –

condolences to caress the swollen eyelids of bleeding
                                        mourners.

the cabinet has gone to hell
the timbers are now on fire
the cabinet that sold itself
ministers are now in gaol –
condolences quivering before the iron throne of a new
conqueror:

the mythmaker accompanies us (*the Egret had come and gone*)
Okigbo accompanies us the oracle enkindles us
the Hornbill is there again (*the Hornbill has had a bath*)
Okigbo accompanies us the rattles enlighten us –

condolences with the miracle of sunlight on our feathers:

The General is up ... the General is up ... commandments ...
the General is up the General is up the General is up –

condolences from our twin-beaks and feathers of condolences:

the General is near the throne
an iron mask covers his face
the General has carried the day
the mortars are far away –

condolences to appease the fever of a wake among tumbled
tombs

the elephant has fallen
the mortars have won the day
the elephant has fallen
does he deserve his fate
the elephant has fallen
can we remember the date –

Jungle tanks blast Britain's last stand –

the elephant ravages the jungle
the jungle is peopled with snakes
the snake says to the squirrel
I will swallow you
the mongoose says to the snake
I will mangle you
the elephant says to the mongoose
I will strangle you

thunder fells the trees cut a path
thunder smashes them all – condolences …

THUNDER that has struck the elephant
the same thunder should wear a plume – condolences

a roadmaker makes a road
the road becomes a throne
can we cane him for felling a tree – condolences …

THUNDER that has struck the elephant
the same thunder can make a bruise – condolences:

we should forget the names
we should bury the date
the dead should bury the dead – condolences

from our bruised lips of the drum empty of condolences:

trunk of the iron tree we cry *condolences* when we break,
shells of the open sea we cry *condolences* when we shake ...

## Elegy for Alto
*With drum accompaniment*

AND THE HORN may now paw the air howling goodbye ...

For the Eagles are now in sight:
Shadows in the horizon –

THE ROBBERS are here in black sudden steps of showers, of
caterpillars –
THE EAGLES have come again,
The eagles rain down on us –

POLITICIANS are back in giant hidden steps of howitzers, of
detonators –
THE EAGLES descend on us,
Bayonets and cannons –

THE ROBBERS descend on us to strip us of our laughter, of our
thunder –
THE EAGLES have chosen their game,
Taken our concubines –

POLITICIANS are here in this iron dance of mortars, of
generators –
THE EAGLES are suddenly there,
New stars of iron dawn;

So let the horn paw the air howling goodbye . . .

O mother mother Earth, unbind me; let this be
my last testament; let this be
The ram's hidden wish to the sword the sword's
secret prayer to the scabbard –

THE ROBBERS are back in black hidden steps of detonators –

FOR BEYOND the blare of sirened afternoons, beyond
 the motorcades;
Beyond the voices and days, the echoing highways: beyond
 the latescence
Of our dissonant airs; through our curtained eyeballs,
 through our shuttered sleep,
Onto our forgotten selves, onto our broken images;
 beyond the barricades
Commandments and edicts, beyond the iron tables,
 beyond the elephant's
Legendary patience, beyond his inviolable bronze
 bust; beyond our crumbling towers –

BEYOND the iron path careering along the same beaten
 track –

THE GLIMPSE of a dream lies smouldering in a cave,
 together with the mortally wounded birds.
Earth, unbind me; let me be the prodigal; let this be
 the ram's ultimate prayer to the tether ...

AN OLD STAR departs, leaves us here on the shore
Gazing heavenward for a new star approaching;
The new star appears, foreshadows its going
Before a going and coming that goes on forever ...